ADULT COLORING BOUK

BY

TATIANA BOGEMA (STOLOVA)

Facebook: Tatiana Bogema (Stolova)

Hi! My name is Tatiana and I'm artist :)
I want to say thank you so much for choosing my books despite the large number of books present on the market. I really appreciate this. Every time I start new project I think about how to make my book mor interesting. And I can't do this without you. To do that I need to have your feedbacks. Communication with you is very very important for creation process. With your feedbacks you give me new ideas and inspiration for new books that become better and more interesting.
Sincerely yours, Tatiana

Christmas - Adult Coloring Book

Copyright © 2019 by Tatiana Bogema (Stolova)

ISBN: 9781695828698

THIS BOOK BELONGS TO

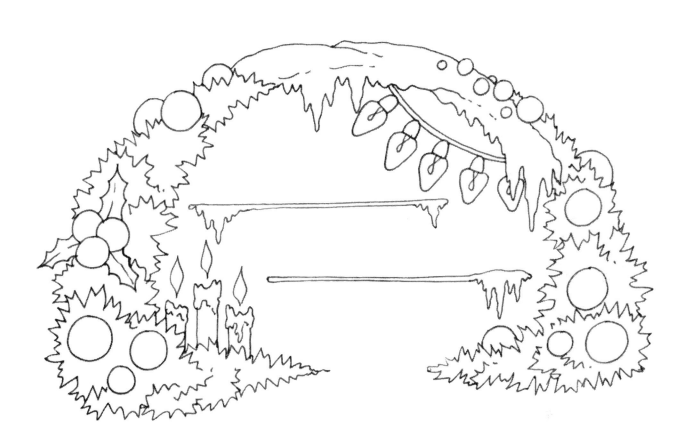

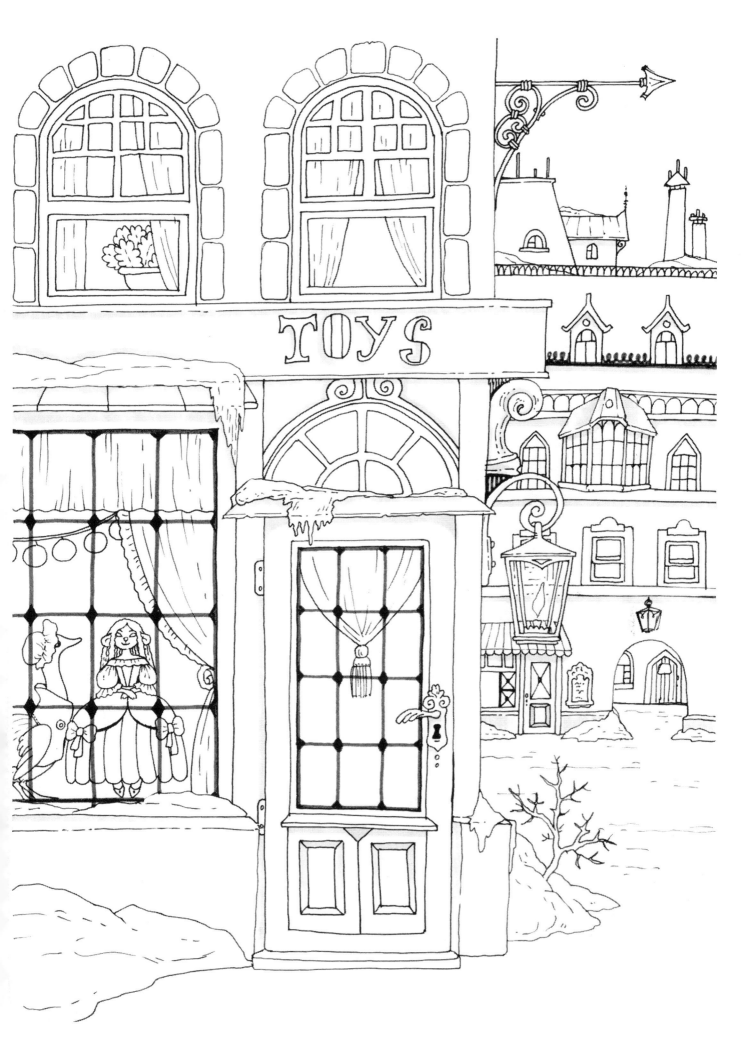

Made in United States
Orlando, FL
06 December 2024

55110175R10037

Three things cannot be long hidden: the sun, the moon, and the truth. Buddha

To become truly great, one has to stand with people, not above them. Montesquieu

Mastering others is strength. Mastering yourself is true power. Laozi

The law is reason, free from passion. Aristotle

To develop courage when you are facing an audience, act as if you already have it.
Dale Carnegie

Be where you are; otherwise you will miss your life. Buddha

All things excellent are as difficult as they are rare. B. Spinoza

When the debate is over, slander becomes the tool of the loser. Socrates

Never do to others what you would not like them to do to you. Confucius

I have never met a man so ignorant that I couldn't learn something from him. Galileo Galilei

Made in the USA
Monee, IL
10 August 2021